Level Five Sales Leader

Field-Tested Strategies to Close the Quota Gap!

John Hoskins
and
Richard Ruff

For more information, email info@levelfiveselling.com.

ISBN: 978-1-64184-485-7

Contents

Dedication

We dedicate this book to all the past and current clients we have served over four decades in our sales consulting practice. Our partnerships with you have allowed us to do the work we love and enhance the lives of thousands of sales leaders and sales professionals while learning from you to keep growing and developing our expertise.

Without you, we would not have been able to share our insights with our readers as well as current and future clients. Thank you for trusting in us to help you meet and exceed your revenue growth targets.

Foreword

For the last thirty-five years, I have had the privilege of consulting with sales leaders worldwide to help them plan their revenue growth strategies, including market segmentation, coverage models, playbooks, messaging, talent assessment, and compensation. In the end, success was about execution. And the frontline sales leader was the critical ingredient in carrying out those plans and overachieving sales goals.

In my opinion, John Hoskins and Richard Ruff have nailed it when it comes to defining attributes of a successful frontline sales leader. Whether you are new to sales leadership or have been a sales leader for several years, this book has something for you. If you are new to sales leadership, the book clarifies what is essential and what is not. If you have been in sales leadership roles for some time, this book provides a great introspective look at what you can do to improve and share your skills with others.

The Level Five Sales Leader model clearly and eloquently lays out a sales leader's normal evolution as they initially enter the role and develop over time. It is easy to see the five sales leader's progression from a "Buddy" ultimately to a "Partner."

The book also captures the three key priorities of a sales leader that will drive long-term business success:

- Always look for new talent and take ownership of building your team's bench strength.
- Understand how to leverage and get the most out of your training initiatives.
- Create an authentic coaching culture, and learn who to coach, what to coach, and how to coach.

Study this book; don't just read it. I assure you that you will take away many great ideas and that you and your sales team will be center stage at the annual awards dinner year after year.

Robert Conti
Senior Vice President
The Alexander Group

Introduction

In 2016, John Hoskins wrote a groundbreaking book called ***Level Five Selling***. Shortly after that, John had a chance meeting with Dick Ruff at their local Starbucks. From that encounter came the idea to translate the book into a new company—Level Five Selling, LLC.

Level Five Selling[1] is the foundational idea that across markets, the days of the price peddler and the product teller is over. Customers want a trusted advisor who can help them create value, not a salesperson who just sells products.

Numerous studies find upward of 50% of salespeople miss their quota. Our field research has validated three disturbing realities:

1. **Scrap and waste.** Sixty percent of all sales calls are scrap and waste. They do not advance a buying decision.
2. **Leading vs. lagging indicators.** Too many sales leaders are focused on managing the pipeline and results versus managing the activities and behaviors that lead to the results.
3. **Less is more.** There is a misplaced emphasis on call quantity versus call quality.

We reprove these findings each time we engage with a new client.

What sales leaders want is a road map to help them build a disciplined approach to improving call quality, not another sales training methodology. They want a blueprint for transforming their sales force into a team who creates unique and innovative value for their customers.

John started to draw that blueprint when he had the great privilege of meeting with Michael Cheek when he was President of Brown-Forman Beverages (think Jack Daniel's) in Louisville, Kentucky.

[1] The Level Five Selling Model is reviewed in the Appendix.

Mike was a former sales leader at The Carnation Company, E&J Gallo Winery, and Coca-Cola. These sales cultures are renowned as disciplined, well-trained, and are considered world-class. Mike had a profound effect on John, which he likely never realized. He said, "John, if we work together, we are going to start by training our sales leaders. I want them to do three things. I want them to be outstanding recruiters, trainers, and coaches."

That engagement led to the development of the Level Five Sales Leader model. The feedback we have received on that model has been overwhelmingly positive. In nearly every instance, clients tell us they want to know more about how they can become a Level Five Sales Leader.

Our learning journey working side by side with frontline sales leaders sent a clear message. If a company expects their sales leaders to meet or exceed their revenue goals, they need to be outstanding recruiters, trainers, and coaches. We, John and Dick, wrote ***The Level Five Sales Leader*** to share our insights gained from our combined decades of sales consulting experience helping sales leaders to achieve that goal.

The Appendix offers many reflection points we have collected from the great sales leaders with whom we have had the privilege of working. Try some out. If you do, we firmly believe you will see dramatic improvements in sales results, less turnover, higher win rates, and more satisfied loyal customers.

Chapter One

The Level Five Sales Leader

> *"Leadership is not magnetic personality—that can just as well be a glib tongue. It is not 'making friends and influencing people'—that is flattery. Leadership is lifting a person's vision to higher sights, the raising of a person's performance to a higher standard, the building of a personality beyond its normal limitations."*
>
> — *Peter F. Drucker*

The Level Five Sales Leadership hierarchy is a conceptual framework that helps us to explore the different styles of leadership based on observations from leaders of frontline sales leaders and sales representatives. This model is useful to establish a context, and it builds a common language and vision for how to lead a high-performing sales team. As a sales leader in a coaching position, explore the model and consider your organization, then ask yourself two questions:

- How am I leading each performer on my team?
- How does each performer feel I am leading them?

Level Five Sales Leader

The Buddy

Feedback must be direct and forthright. The Level One leader tends to let things ride to preserve the relationship and believes the false narrative that friendship breeds success. Sadly, that ride takes the team down the road to failure as performance problems fester and become harder to correct.

The Buddy approach can be summarized as follows:

- If they like me, they will perform.
- They are slow to let underperformers go.
- Underestimates the potential upside of developmental feedback.
- Believes candid feedback will harm the friendship.
- They get uncomfortable when performance falls below expectations.
- Tends to let things ride versus confront them.
- Rarely follows any routine-disciplined process; wings it.
- Is happy with the status quo; avoids conflict of any kind.

"I cannot give you the formula for success, but I can give you the formula for failure, which is: Try to please everybody."

— *Herbert B. Swope*

The Parent

At some point, a leader learns that being best buddies doesn't drive results. Now the leader takes a more directive approach by providing suggestions and encouragement. But the communications and interactions are still based on a personal peer relationship.

The Parent approach can be summarized as follows:

- They ignore their team's limitations. My baby is not ugly.
- May tend to hire salespeople from their previous "family" (company).
- Overly protective. If they fail, it's a reflection on me.
- Stifles individual learning; shelters salesperson from adversity.
- Few actions can be taken without the permission of the Parent.
- Creates a culture of dependency.
- Will do the job for them to avoid letting someone go. After all, it's one of my children.

"High sentiments always win in the end; the leaders who offer blood, toil, tears, and sweat always get more out of their followers than those who offer safety and a good time. When it comes to the pinch, human beings are heroic."

— *George Orwell*

The Boss

This approach accomplishes the little it manages to achieve by compliance with rules and dictates from the leader, not from a sense of commitment derived from a shared vision for personal growth between the leader and salesperson.

The Boss approach can be summarized as follows:

- Driven primarily by a "do as you're told" style.
- Hires in their image; uses gut feel and looks for the Yes Sir/ Madam attitude.
- Little give and take; coaching dialogues are "tell versus ask."
- The Boss focuses on correcting deficiencies versus leveraging a player's strengths.
- They devalue individual differences. It's best if everyone uses the same approach to their job.
- Creates a culture that discourages initiative.
- Uses process to a fault; micromanages every action and decision.

"People ask the difference between a leader and a boss. The leader leads, and the boss drives."

— *Theodore Roosevelt*

The Expert Coach

As the label implies, the Expert Coach exhibits the behaviors and skills required for the first level of professional coaching. While the Expert Coach does suggest performance changes tailored to the individual members of the sales team, communication is one-sided.

The Expert Coach approach can be summarized as follows:

- Has the expertise/knowledge to provide value.
- Recognizes the value of diverse skills for different jobs.
- Takes training and practice seriously.
- Tailors advice to the individual.
- Talks 80% of the time and listens only 20%.
- One-way communication may lead to resentment.
- Performance improvement is based on compliance, not commitment.

- When performance fails, it's never the Expert Coach's fault.
- Might tolerate toxic salespeople if they ring the revenue bell.
- May rely on a single profile or type when hiring.

"The mediocre teacher tells. The good teacher explains. The superior teacher demonstrates. The great teacher inspires."

— *William Arthur Ward*

The Partner

A Partner employs a collaborative approach to leading; they ask more than they tell. This shifts from the Level Four approach of "I'm the expert, and I'll diagnose what's wrong and suggest what you should develop" to "You're the one responsible for development. I'm responsible for helping you become more aware of your performance and expanding your developmental choices."

The Partner approach can be summarized as follows:

- The communication shifts from "I" and "You" to "We."
- Is always sourcing new talent; recruits only the best skilled who fit a diverse culture.
- Sets the tone by aligning the team to a shared vision, mission, and core values.
- Develops a mutual understanding of development through inquiry and listening versus telling.
- Builds self-awareness and self-confidence.
- Develops salespeople who are committed.
- Reinforces strengths but is candid and straightforward when referencing deficiencies.
- Is consistent in attitude and actions; follows a routine process.

"To lead people, walk beside them ... As for the best leaders, the people do not notice their existence. The next best, the people honor and praise. The next, the people fear; and the next, the people hate ... When the best leader's work is done the people say, 'We did it ourselves!'"

— *Lao Tzu*

Summary

Invariably we've found that leaders admit to leading team members at all different levels. Few, if any, were able to say they were at the Partner level with each direct report, not to mention the leadership level they were on with their own leader.

In all aspects of selling, the notion of a common language makes good sense. It applies to pipeline management, sales strategy, and planning and executing sales calls—it also applies to leadership.

The Level Five Leadership hierarchy provides both sales leaders and salespeople an easy-to-use common language for assessing and improving their working relationship, which in turn impacts morale and results.

Sales leaders know a lot about the art and science of selling. The trick is how you can tap into that experience to help your sales team improve their performance. For sure you can't get there merely by telling salespeople, "You need to do more of this and less of that." Changing sales behavior requires a very skilled leader. Many activities can pull a sales leader in different directions and burden them with low payback tasks. However, we believe those who recruit and retain the best talent, invest in training, and have well-practiced coaching skills to reinforce the training are the leaders who can become the developmental Level Five Partners.

Reflection Point 1

PAUSE FOR NOW AND COMPLETE THE EXERCISE ON PAGE 61

Chapter Two

The Sales Leader as Recruiter

"The best executive is the one who has sense enough to pick good people to do what he wants done, and self-restraint to keep from meddling with them while they do it."

— *Theodore Roosevelt*

Finding and Attracting the Best Sales Talent

Hiring managers in any functional area can lead to pain when a bad hire is made. This story from a close colleague and partner is telling. It is about a conversation he had with an SVP of engineering for a huge global aerospace company.

During his final presentation pursuing a six-figure assessment services contract, he made this point about the process and service he was recommending: "Our firm will help you hire the best engineers in the country."

The SVP abruptly stopped his pitch and interjected. "Look," he said. "There are not enough great engineers out there to fill my demand for talent." He continued, "What I want you to do is help me not hire any bad engineers. We simply cannot afford that mistake."

Similar to hiring a bad engineer, hiring a bad salesperson will have its acute pain and long-lasting side effects as well.

Some time ago, we observed a workshop on behavioral interviewing. The participants were seasoned and, we might add, a talented group of frontline sales leaders (over three hundred years of cumulative expertise in a room of twenty). To warm them up and set the context for the day, the facilitator asked them to work individually to think of a time when they made a poor hiring decision.

The facilitator asked them to share their thoughts and describe the costs or business impact of that hire.

The list of comments was long; however, the themes were consistent. There ended up being several "impact and cost" buckets.

- Low team morale/manager credibility
- Time drain for the manager, manager's manager, and HR
- Customers poorly served; loss of goodwill
- It tarnished the company and managers' reputation and brand
- Recruiting costs increased
- Sales opportunities were lost
- Legal and severance costs increased
- The person felt like a failure; it was a career-damaging experience

Next, they were to consider the characteristics of one of their organization's best hires—again, working on their own and then sharing answers with the group. Once more, this exercise produced very similar responses.

Best Hires

Like the first question, the themes are consistent. These characteristics, summarized in similar categories to those listed above, are nearly opposites.

- Contributed to the team morale/credibility
- Did not drain time for the manager, manager's manager, or HR; took the initiative and enjoyed the challenge
- Passionate about the customers and eagerly served them to build goodwill
- Company and managers' reputation and brand were enhanced by the person's presence, not diminished
- Recruiting costs decreased
- Sales opportunities win rates improved
- Avoid significant legal and severance expense
- The people themselves added value to the team, customers, and the organization

Hiring the Right Talent Is a Sales Leader's Cure-All

We asked dozens of frontline and senior executive sales leaders to suppose they had only one thing they could do to increase the odds of making quota. What would it be? The answer was unanimous: Finding and keeping the best sales talent wins the game. The team that gets and nurtures the most A players wins! Most added a powerful exclamation point. End of sentence. Full stop.

Numerous research studies continue to report that upward of 50% of salespeople fail to meet assigned sales targets.

We don't like to argue with success or experience; we also believe that the team who makes fewer unforced hiring errors wins the game. The message is that you can be nearly 100% assured of building the best sales team and yielding those above-average revenue results if you apply a rigorous process to building and maintaining your sales talent pipelines using our seven habits.

Seven Habits of Highly Successful Sales Recruiters

Habit 1: ABR—Always Be Recruiting!

Our overarching premise is a simple one, and something sales leaders have always instinctively known. It is the single most potent habit of the seven.

To explain it, we've borrowed from David Mamet's 1984 Pulitzer Prize-winning and Tony Award-nominated play, *Glengarry Glen Ross.* In the movie version, Alec Baldwin plays the sales leader, Blake, who chides his team with the dated mantra, "ABC—Always Be Closing." We offer sales leaders an updated version; ours is ABR—Always Be Recruiting.

John first learned this lesson while at Xerox, in the Chicago branch. A fellow sales leader, Russ Paterra, had made a superstar hire in Minneapolis, and John remembers asking him:

"Where did you find that guy? Was he from an external recruiter, our HR group, an advertisement in *The Wall Street Journal*?"

"Nope. Found him in a hotel lobby standing in line to check in."

"What? You must be joking!"

He smiled. "Nope. I know one when I see one, so I asked him what he did, and he told me. I told him what we did, and we exchanged cards. That was more than a year ago. I've been nursing him along all this time. He finally got dissatisfied with his current job, and today he's my numero uno."

- **Habit-Forming Action Step**
  Think of recruiting like how a good salesperson thinks of prospecting. You always have to keep your ear to the ground and be looking for the next hire.

Habit 2: Engage and partner with your sales recruiters.

Many sales leaders have told us that their relationship with internal and external sales recruiters was not ideal. Why? Because sales leaders complain of a trickle of candidates, many of whom are not qualified and, therefore, waste their interviewing time. Sales recruiters we've spoken with are likewise dissatisfied with the responsiveness of sales leaders. The leaders postpone interviews, don't communicate promptly when a good prospect appears on the radar, and can't articulate in detail what they're looking for in a top performer.

Unfortunately, many sales leaders and their recruiting partners also cling to an "abundance" recruiting mindset and process. Even though supply is scarce, they believe there are plenty of rock star salespeople out there, "so we'll look for them when we need them." (Remember Habit 1? Always Be Recruiting!)

All these issues speak to a lack of precision in both expectations and recruiting processes.

- **Habit-Forming Action Step**
  Add more communication, attention, and precision in your internal processes, and you'll turn your recruiting efforts around. Your HR staff can't help unless you routinely reach out to collaborate with them.

Habit 3: Inspect what you expect.

You've heard it a million times: If you can't or don't measure it, you can't manage it. Recruiting—unlike call activity, forecast updates, or expense reports—isn't something due on Friday at five o'clock. In the best situations, you review it quarterly. In the worst, not until turnover forces the issue.

The lesson here is like the old FRAM oil filter ad slogan: "You can pay me now, or pay me later." Sales leaders often ignore a daily recruiting routine because "I don't need to. I have all my territories filled." Sales leaders make this assumption at their own peril.

Turnover happens when you least expect it and generally when you are unprepared for it. When you inspect what you expect, you know what the sales talent pipeline looks like, and you don't get caught off guard when your best salesperson walks in your office with a smile—and resigns.

- **Habit-Forming Action Step**
  Set up weekly or monthly recruiting pipeline reviews that use probabilities to determine where you are in your sales process and where the candidate is in their buying process. Good players have options, and you need to consider recruiting a half-buy, half-sell process.

Habit 4: Embed "just in case" accountability.

Just in time (JIT) may be a best practice for lean manufacturing inventory and financial metrics, but it's a worst practice for recruiting. Just in case (JIC) is a better mindset.

Sales talent management is the one place in a business where a JIC inventory process means dollars and makes sense. You don't carry the inventory of "candidates-in-waiting" on your balance sheet like raw materials. They are intangible assets, a more contemporary measurement of an organization's health, much like recruiting brand and employee engagement.

Sales superstars are not commodities. They don't show up on your doorstep when you have an open territory. You have to apply Habit 1 (Always Be Recruiting!) to find those A players. And you'd better have a "just in case" contingency plan in your mind.

- **Habit-Forming Action Step**
  Require sales leaders to report quarterly on the probability of turnover for every salesperson in their district. In addition, list a minimum of two names and phone numbers of backup candidates they would call tomorrow if a salesperson was to turn over unexpectedly. (And they do!)

Habit 5: Define "what good looks like" using objective, scientific success predictors.

We see it all the time: Recruiting strategies have no destination in mind, and tactics are all over the subjective map. That's no way to run a railroad—or a sales organization.

Whether starting up a sales team, growing one, or replacing turnover, you need a recruiting plan. It starts with a precise picture of what a good sales performer looks like. Yet, even that clear description is only one part of the prescription for a healthy talent pipeline.

For example, an extensive study by The HR Chally Group of more than one thousand sales superstars from seventy companies showed that these high achievers believed the top three characteristics required for good salesmanship were:

1. Strong objection-answering skills
2. Good grooming
3. Conservative dress (especially black shoes)

However, a study of the weakest performers at these companies revealed that these same three characteristics were also their most common traits. Hence, this is not the way to recruit a sales star.

In reality, few criteria for selection are better than many, and one or two factors typically account for more than 80% of a salesperson's ability to succeed in a specific role.

- **Habit-Forming Action Step**
  Defining your target hiring requirements means more than gathering people in a room to identify top-performer competencies. In these meetings, the opinion voiced loudest often dominates. You need more than advice to predict success. You need science in the mix to be objective about what you are looking for versus using subjective criteria to pick a superstar.

Habit 6: Increase behavioral interviewing "at-bats" with job aids and practice.

When you examine how you recruit and manage sales talent, how many times are you "at-bat"? Do you know—or care? You should. Malcolm Gladwell, in his bestselling book *Outliers*, suggests that ten thousand hours of effort is the point at which you approach mastery.

With sales recruiting, sales leaders get rusty when they interview infrequently. Behavioral interviewing training is standard fare in sales management curricula. But if you interview candidates only a few times a year, you do get rusty.

When you're rusty and have to make decisions under pressure to fill a quota-bearing territory (which you are likely covering in your spare time), anyone who can fog a mirror could walk through your office and look like the perfect salesperson! Need we say it? This habit leads to unforced hiring errors. "Time to fill" is often stated as a metric to measure the effectiveness of recruiters. Unfortunately, it also leads to bad decisions due to a rush to judgment to hit a lagging indicator metric.

- **Habit-Forming Action Step**
  Set an interview activity target just like you would establish a sales call activity target. At a minimum, interview a new candidate either by phone or face-to-face once a week. Take time to prepare properly and use the same standard for evaluating the interview as you would an effective sales call. You should talk 20% of the time and the candidate 80%.

Habit 7: Check the DNA before the resume.

Resumes are candidates' bold-faced attempts to reflect their best possible image to an employer. A resume is an undeniably flawed input; studies have shown that most of them are riddled with half-truths. The professional social site LinkedIn claims to have improved that percentage because its resumes are accessible online and can be questioned or verified publicly. But according to HireRight, a firm that specializes in employee background checks:

- 85% of all employers report finding that resumes are misleading
- 29% state fraudulent degrees
- 30% show altered employment dates
- 40% have inflated salary claims
- 30% have inaccurate job descriptions
- 27% give falsified references

Not only is a resume pile imperfect input to begin with, but the fact remains that resumes are the least reliable method of screening for quality.

- **Habit-Forming Action Step**
  When selecting which resumes you choose, using unscientific data quickly leads to false positives or indicators and markers that are subjective. Worse is using no data at all; most sales recruiters we talk to say their clients don't know what they're looking for precisely. Suddenly, that's your selection criteria. And for every excellent candidate you select, you may be losing an even better one.

Since resumes are the least reliable method of screening for quality, it's no wonder sales leaders complain of not enough qualified candidates. To prove the point, just ask yourself, "Why did those hires who didn't work out have such great looking resumes?" You can't judge a book by its cover, and yet sales recruiters do it day in and day out.

Full disclosure: John also owns a sales assessment company, so he is biased toward them. Use predictive assessments to avoid the pitfalls of relying on resumes and interviews alone in your decision-making.

Build Bench Strength

By routinely applying these seven habits as part of your recruiting process, you will build bench strength. Having a bench of qualified candidates is an excellent elixir for many sales ailments.

For example, when you ponder the reluctance of frontline sales leaders to let people who aren't performing go, it is as though they believe "the devil you know" in a sales territory is better than "the devil you don't." How about building your bench strength so you need not be reluctant to let poor performers go in the first place?

Admittedly, building a backup is sometimes met with questions or objections. At Xerox, we used to visit different districts where sales leaders and salespeople alike would ask, "Why are you interviewing people in this territory today? Do you think I'm leaving? Are you planning to split my territory? Are you going to replace me?" We suggest you answer them directly and explain that, to you, "chance" is not a strategy. Anything can happen, "and if I don't have a backup for you, I'm out of luck." That usually prompts a healthy conversation about career aspirations, their happiness quotient (they call it "engagement" these days), and the probability that they might take another job offer. These are good conversations to engage in proactively before it's too late.

When you probe sales leaders about their pipeline during quarterly reviews, many complain that it is hard to keep good candidates on ice. Although that's true, it's far better that you stay connected with that person over the long haul than to allow them to slip by—and away—when you aren't actively looking for someone. You wouldn't think of putting a customer prospect in your pipeline and not drip-feeding your frequent contact to keep them warm. The same applies to recruiting top talent.

What do lost effective sales months* cost?

Want a real eye-opener? Calculate and track the overall impact of letting salespeople go without anybody to step into their position. Say your $100 million business has 100 sales territories, each with a $1 million sales quota. Assume 15% turnover. If you have no recruitment best practices in place—and if you're lucky—it will take you three months to fill each territory with a full-time salesperson and six more months to get them up to speed. So, those 15 territories lose nine effective sales months each, or 135 effective sales months total. At about $83.3k per month, you must require another $132k per salesperson from the remaining 85 salespeople to meet the quota. Even if some repeat business flows in representing half the quota of each open territory, you'll still need one additional effective sales month's revenue from every salesperson to make your bonus—not a formula for success.

* To calculate the value of an effective sales month, multiply the total number of FTE salespeople you have in territory times 12. Divide your full-year quota (budget/revenue target) by that number. That indicates the average revenue per month, per salesperson you must achieve to make your sales goal.

Making the Big Decision

Sales leaders who lose a salesperson are under pressure to perform. Quotas don't go away. The VP doesn't say, "Oh, don't worry about that territory's number. I got you covered. I'll lower your target for the year." Bob Means, a sage in the field of sales recruiting, once described this pressure:

When an open slot in the team occurs, it almost always pressures the hiring manager to find any candidate fast. The manager knows that if they don't fill the territory quickly, the odds of making bonus, going on this year's incentive award trip, and being on stage at the annual sales meeting are fading away. The theme song becomes Z.Z. Top's "Got Me Under Pressure."

When deciding to hire a new salesperson, you can't be overly deliberate, or you might lose the opportunity to hire great talent. However, your process and due diligence must go beyond gut feel and winging it as the consequences are too ominous.

At Level Five, we encourage clients to use the 25-25-25-25 decision-making model.

Selling Skills – Twenty-five percent of your decision should validate the selling skills the person possesses. Are those the skills you know lead to success in the unique type of selling you do? Can they do what you need them to do? We often discuss turnover with frontline sales leaders, and they have a refrain: "Well, we hired Mike for who he was, and everyone really liked him. But I had to fire him for what he couldn't do." That means he lacked the fundamental sales skills to succeed. Find a validated sales assessment tool that will help you measure skills you can observe, train, and coach to. Personality tests are not reliable predictors of sales success. Look for a tool that is validated, EEOC-compliant, and is accurate and reliable at predicting success. If it doesn't give you a reliable "hire or don't hire" recommendation, then you are using a less than optimal tool.

Behavioral Interviews – Twenty-five percent of the decision should weigh the individual's performance in interviews. As we described in Habit 6, make sure each person interviewing the candidate is using an interview guide that directs the conversation by asking in-depth questions about the candidate's past performance. Make sure people in the process are planning for their interview and prepare to debrief with you afterward. Don't just rely on the person giving you a thumbs-up answer when you ask them how it went. Get specifics and compare those details to the profile you are seeking to hire. Recently, we read that the odds of making the right decision increase if at least nine people interview the candidate. Some candidates will push back, but ask yourself why they might be in such a hurry.

Background Checks and Reference Checks – Twenty-five percent should be based on thorough background checks and reference checks. This step is getting harder and harder to do. Regulations restrict employers from giving any information beyond the dates the person was employed and the position they held. There are professional background check services, and they tend to be the way to go today. References are "feel-good calls" as the smart candidate isn't going to tell you anything wrong even if you ask, "So what are your weaknesses?" Answer: She works way too hard. One manager we know would ask for the candidate's top two references, and then after speaking to them, they would ask for two more. His premise was the first two were the best. Today, with LinkedIn, you can do some searching around for others who work at the same company. Let's put it this way—you must play the part of a detective to make sure there aren't shortcomings you've overlooked. Use your imagination and stay within the law.

Culture and Values – Twenty-five percent of your conclusion about the candidate is whether they fit your culture. Are they aligned with your core values and the cadence of your organization's process? Do they share a passion for the company or team vision, and will they be a net add to the team? This is an essential part of your organization's value proposition to talented players. The well-known shoe and apparel company Zappos (now an Amazon company) had to hire 250 customer care reps in Las Vegas. The job paid $11 an hour, yet their culture was so highly regarded that they received 25,000 applicants to fill the slots.

What About Gut Feel?

No matter what anyone says, sales leaders make gut-feel decisions. The problem is trying to quantify a gut feeling. Interviews are an unnatural meeting environment, especially when a motivated buyer (the sales leader) is meeting with a motivated seller (the candidate). Over the years, we've found that there are some good questions to ask yourself whenever making this chemistry-check decision. Try these out on your next hiring decision. Credit goes to the many sales leaders we know who taught us these key checkpoints:

- Are you excited about hiring this person? Do you feel a sense of excitement and energy that makes you eager to bring them into the team? If you are not excited now, you never will be.
- Is this someone you would invite over to your home for dinner? This one sounds a bit corny, but if you don't want to introduce them to your family, doesn't that tell you something?
- Would you buy from this person? If this individual called on you to sell you *anything*—a car, a house, maybe even your product—do you see yourself buying from them?
- Do you see this person with the company five years from now? A job hopper is a job hopper. A manager of John's at Xerox used to say that any applicant with more than three sales jobs in five years was a noncontender. The exception was upwardly mobile salespeople in the same company who went from inside sales to a territory and then to major accounts or sales management.
- Do they have a trail of blue ribbons? This is equivalent to reading the racing form. The same Xerox manager wanted everything from the top seller of Girl Scout cookies to five years in a row as a member of President's Club. Winners tend to win over and over. You need to look for accomplishments where they excel at what they do over time.

In summary, avoiding costly hiring mistakes requires a consistent approach to your selection process. Consider the many possible tools you can employ to source, screen, assess, and select a new hire. The more rigor and discipline you can put into the process, the more likely you will have the desired outcome, and the higher the probability that you will make your quota, attend this year's incentive trip and, of course, cash that bonus check at the end of the year.

Good Hiring!

One last piece of advice: If you happen to make a bad hiring decision, cut your losses early. We'd venture to say that most of us know we made a mistake within a few weeks, maybe even a few days. If you suspect that you were somehow fooled and there are early warning signs and symptoms that you goofed, don't hang on for hope. Certainly, you must follow whatever HR guidelines you are accountable to, but don't let your decision to fire linger, hoping things will get better. Trust your instincts; they are likely right. Clients tell me the worst managers are quick to hire and slow to fire. Sounds like The Buddy or The Parent to me.

Reflection Point 2

PAUSE FOR NOW AND COMPLETE THE EXERCISE ON PAGE 63

Chapter Three

The Sales Leader as Trainer

What Every Sales Leader Should Know About Sales Training

> *"Training is appropriate only when two conditions are present: (1) there is something that one or more people don't know how to do, and (2) they need to be able to do it."*
>
> — *Dr. Robert Mager*

According to a study by Training Industry, global corporations spend north of $355 billion a year training their people.

Sales training is estimated at $2.46 billion. While this amount is a small portion of the total, it is still a lot of money. It seems that companies make most of this investment in good faith without any solid proof of a return on investment.

Why Bother?

Recently, a colleague stated that he believed there are two kinds of people in the world. There are those who believe in sales training and those who do not. Unlike other areas of training, the tangible results of sales training can be tracked. Metrics such as more salespeople making quota, reduced time to productivity, better win-loss ratios, and increased levels of customer satisfaction can provide useful feedback about the effectiveness of the training. Too few companies optimize their efforts to evaluate their sales training either from a formative or summative perspective. It may be, in many cases, the lifetime value of just a few new accounts will more than pay for the expense associated with the effort.

Also, the intangible value provides more rationale to double down on your future training investments.

Here are three "intangible value" examples:

1. **Improved Recruiting Brand**
   Every sales leader wants to hire top performers. Your recruiting brand is key. Companies that have a reputation for providing great training enjoy the benefits of attracting the best talent to their team more easily. When John was a frontline sales leader at Xerox, there was always a steady stream of resumes every week. Of course, the firm did not rely on that reputation exclusively to source candidates. Other items included actively advertising, using internal and external recruiters, and promoting a robust referral program with large bounties when a new hire accepted an offer and stayed for one year. Yet, the intangible value does not end there.

2. **Reduced Turnover**
   At the time, Xerox offered a continuous stream of learning about selling and sales management. Not a quarter went by without exposure to reinforcement sessions for practice or netting new content to build on your foundation of mastering sales. Hence, the engagement level was high, success was common, and rewards were handsome. Turnover was, at a minimum, the biggest payback, which meant more customers benefited from fewer "revolving-door-reps" in their accounts. This led to more repeat business and fewer competitive inroads.

3. **Increased Number of Satisfied Customers**
   Customer expectations are higher than ever before. Customers do not want to waste their time with salespeople who do not create value for them. Sending in unskilled neophyte salespeople to make calls does more harm than good. It would serve companies better not to have them practice on their customers. Tim Riesterer, Chief Strategy Officer at Corporate Visions, says, "At some point in the

sales process, lips have to move." Your customers stand in judgment of whether your salespeople create value. Skilled salespeople are invited to come into an account; unskilled ones are avoided like the plague. If you depend heavily on repeat business and expanding relationships, you want your best foot forward in those key accounts. Training—in fact, *overtraining*—keeps salespeople one step ahead of the competition, earning that customer's business for life.

Five Best Practices

Whether you are a sales leader who believes in training or one who does not, here are five best practices to maximize your return on the investment regardless of how much you spend. These practices may turn skeptics into believers and positively influence C-level support for further investment in the future.

1. **Be a partner, not a customer.**
   Management oversight, involvement, and shared accountability with sales training are critical success factors for achieving the best results from your sales training investment.

   Sales leadership needs to see their relationship with sales enablement as a partnership. You own it anyway. Because sales leadership will be on point at the end of the year, take the lead from the beginning. Start by frequently communicating with your sales enablement team. Get involved and stay involved throughout the process. Meet with everyone on your team before they attend training to set expectations and shared outcomes. Then, meet with them after training to plan how to coach and reinforce what has been learned so it can be applied and transferred back to the job.

   We advocate that frontline sales leaders become true sales leaders when they are involved in the delivery of the training and the follow-up and reinforcement of the same.

2. Prescription without diagnosis is malpractice.

"Good trainers can guarantee skill, but they can't guarantee on-the-job performance."

— Dr. Robert Mager

Many things can be learned from Dr. Rob Brinkerhoff, guru on training evaluation and measurement. He has many sage one-liners. One of those includes, "Sales leaders tend to order training like they order pizza." There is a tendency to turn to the sales enablement department when performance is not meeting expectations and order a program.

Training is not always the answer. Do not believe for one second that training will fix them or make them better like a doctor would. Conduct a needs analysis, and not just a standard topical training needs analysis. Participate and practice a performance-based needs analysis.

Review some form of the model by the International Society for Performance Improvement (ISPI) on human performance technology (HPT). For example, Dr. Carl Binder's Six Boxes model is an excellent way to diagnose a performance challenge. He recommends you examine a myriad of other performance influences to determine the root cause of the performance gap before concluding it is time to invest in training. At a macro level, we believe you should ask yourself:

- Have I communicated what I want the performer to accomplish?
- Do they know my appraisal of their performance? Is it shared?
- Are there assets available to them to enable their performance?
- Do they have adequate skill level to perform?
- Are they in the right role?
- Do they have the desire or willingness to perform?

- Are there sufficient consequences for performing well or not well?

Once you have determined that training can move the needle, it is time to decide the content, methods, and strategy for implementation, evaluation, and measurement. What behaviors will change? Will they grow revenue? Don't forget to involve the salesperson in the process.

Finally, incorporate some client feedback on your salespeople in the analysis and do some in-field observations to know the current state-of-call behavior. The approach to field observation is detailed in John's book, *Level Five Coaching System.*

3. **Select the right content.**
   Do not be swayed by the next new, shiny object in sales training. Believe me, plenty of prospects have spent a ton of money and saw no discernable difference from what they did last year. We call it the Sales Training Parade.

There are three reasons that the parade has happened in many organizations. The primary reason is the absence of follow-up and reinforcement. This includes frequent call observation and deep, deliberate practice of the skills and processes taught. The second contributor to the parade is flawed methodology. Two- or three-day events are not the way of the future. We know most of what is learned is forgotten within thirty days. You need ongoing learning journeys where there is continuous improvement. Finally, the third reason is a lack of senior leadership support in holding the frontline responsible and accountable for sticking with it.

Avoid selecting an efficiency solution when you have an effectiveness problem and vice versa. Suppose the following: The sales team would sell more if they made more face-to-face calls, and you have an efficiency problem. This stands to reason. If they managed their time and territory better, they would spend more time in front of customers. It would be like, "Ordering, one-time management program, hold the cheese." For post-training, you determine the sales team made 15% more calls next quarter. Guess what? Sales did not improve, and there was no funnel growth. Making numerous poor-quality calls (effectiveness) does not ever lead to more sales.

Here is another common example. This is a classic. Margins are shrinking, and the client says, "We need negotiation skills." Really? Could it be your salespeople do not know how to sell at Level Five and create value so they are getting cost objections?

"Efficiency is doing things right; effectiveness is doing the right things."

— Peter F. Drucker

Be sure to customize the content.

The materials and content must be tailored to your business, products, market segments, and competition. Asking a learner to acquire new knowledge and translate it to your business is ineffective. They need to immediately see the content relevance and connect the skill or process to their job. This aids in transfer and accelerates behavior change.

Avoid one-size-fits-all events where everyone gets the same program.

Today, it is possible not only to customize the training to your company or division but also to personalize it to the individual salesperson. The difference in the receptivity from the learners and the final measurable results is significant.

People do not need to learn content they are already skilled in—that is a matter of fine-tuning and coaching. Others may not have the foundational skills in place to learn a new, more advanced skill.

In other cases, it is simply a skill that does not fit well with the salesperson's overall competency. The classic is teaching salespeople who are great farmers to prospect for new business. It is not what they are good at or like doing. You can hover over them, and they might do it. However, once you are not there, they will not do it. Individual learning tracks are best. Don't try to make the squirrel fly and swim and the duck climb trees and bury nuts.

4. **Utilize line-driven, drip-fed learning methodologies.** No salesperson should be asked to attend a training program that his leader has not attended previously or participated in simultaneously. The best of all possible worlds is where the sales leader participates in the facilitation of the program. Having them fluent in the content, whether it is skills or process, adds credibility to the program and arms them to coach and reinforce the desired behaviors. Some of the best VP of Sales clients were not the ones who showed up, introduced the program, and went back to their desks and meetings. They showed up, stayed, and used the training as a laboratory for observing their team's behaviors. They participated and did not lead from behind.

Design learning to be consumed in small bite-sized chunks and drip-fed over time versus the method of flooding the field irrigation. The latter creates learning events that are short-lived and ineffective. The former accelerates the transfer, sustains retention, and increases applications and transfer. Better to learn a few things well and master them than taking the waterfront approach to curriculum designs that cover every topic under the sun. Add action-oriented projects and refreshers along the way to keep the concepts in the forefront as part of the sales culture.

5. **Evaluate and measure results.**
   If you want senior leaders to continue to fund the development of your team, connect learning to the business impact. This is much easier than people make it out to be. Documenting bottom-line results helps you compete in the battle for investment spending when the CFO is looking at the trade-offs of those who want a big share of the pie. If faced with purchasing a new software program or buying a piece of capital equipment, the CFO will have an ROI analysis in front of them. If you present your training budget without those compelling returns, the odds are slim to none that you will get the money you want.

   Start training by first committing to an evaluation and measurement process to prove your ROI. Publish those results broadly, so no one doubts the value created by you and your partner in training.

Conclusion

Many other factors can guarantee a payback from your training investments. These are just a few of them. However, simply putting these practices in place will increase the odds of getting sales results from the training investments you make now and in the future.

Reflection Point 3

PAUSE FOR NOW AND COMPLETE THE EXERCISE ON PAGE 64

CHAPTER FOUR

The Sales Leader as Coach

Getting Serious About Coaching

Senior leadership talks about it all the time. Management consultants advocate it. The "it" is building a Coaching Culture. Sales leaders also say they would like to do more coaching if they had the time.

When we nose around out there, we often find less coaching is occurring than might be expected, given all the voices of advocacy. Why might that be? Well, there are several reasons, but four of the more devilish are:

- **Conflicting demands.** Sales leaders are the key for great coaching, but the problem is they get bogged down doing all sorts of special ancillary projects and administrative things. Coaching gets put off until Friday, and it never happens, and nobody is measuring to know if it is happening.
- **Great numbers.** Last quarter's numbers get tabulated, and they look okay. So, the impetus to get serious about coaching tends to wane, and any serious effort is postponed to next quarter or until a devastating set of revenue numbers appear.
- **Zombie ideas.** Sometimes bad ideas just won't die. In this case, notions keep coming back to life in the corporate culture like: "We have an experienced sales team, so coaching is not really a necessity" or "We're okay on the coaching thing; our leaders talk with our salespeople all the time."
- **Seduction.** Some new bright and shiny object distracts the sales leadership and commitment to the coaching effort is lost. Without that leadership, coaching does not happen in a pervasive fashion.

In many companies, not much coaching is occurring, but folks seem immobilized to do anything about it. So, the questions are: Does it really matter? Is coaching really a big deal? Is it a must-do priority? The clear answer to each question is *yes*!

> *A 2019 research study by Gartner asked forty-seven chief sales officers to select the top three initiatives most critical to their organization's success in 2020. The number one answer to the poll was "improving sales manager effectiveness."*

In case you get tasked to craft a PowerPoint presentation to convince others to get serious about coaching, here are five reasons why the idea is a good one:

1. **Shows leadership commitment.** It demonstrates that the top sales leadership is serious about providing support for developing the strength of the sales team and for the professional development of the individual members of the team.
2. **Coaches get smarter.** If sales leaders increase the amount of time they spend coaching, they will get smarter about their sales teams and the customer base. They will be better able to serve as an effective early warning system of changes in the market and what to do about it.
3. **Leverages knowledge.** Think of the cumulative knowledge possessed by the sales leaders in an organization. Coaching provides an effective and efficient approach for leveraging that knowledge to the sales team. Without coaching, that knowledge is lost if a sales leader leaves the organization.
4. **Reinforces sales training.** The research indicates that approximately 87% of the skill-gain in a sales training program is lost in three months without reinforcement. Without a doubt, coaching is the most effective method to reinforce the skills learned in sales training.
5. **Grows the business.** A better-skilled sales team is an important piece of the puzzle for generating increased revenue and optimizing profits.

So, is coaching necessary? The answer is still a resounding *yes*! Lots of good things happen when a company gets it right, and unfortunately, some bad things occur when they don't. For additional evidence of the power of coaching, see the Appendix and our white paper, which summarizes a variety of independent research studies completed that provide examples of significant sales results from coaching initiatives.

Two additional developments increase the urgency for a renewed dialogue about getting coaching right:

> **Sales-team performance is a bigger piece of the competitive advantage puzzle.** Presently, it is extremely difficult to sustain a competitive advantage by product alone. Even if you have a winning product, the competition is likely to get a product to market that is just as good, at half the price—in half the time it took several years ago. Although a superior sales team is extremely difficult to assemble and train, once you have one, it is one of the few sustainable advantages left.
>
> **Sales excellence is more difficult to achieve.** Not only is superior sales performance more important than ever; it's harder to get there. Today, salespeople must develop their knowledge and skills to an unprecedented level. Now top performers must know more and know it at a higher level of competency than ever before. Today, customers expect salespeople to be advisors they can trust, not product facilitators. In many companies, a substantial number of the top performers ten years ago would not make the cut for this year's President's Club.

Summary

It is more important than ever to have a superior sales team. At Level Five, a sales team can sell in person or virtually. Unfortunately, achieving that goal is a much greater challenge than in years past. Consequently, market-leading companies are taking a second look at getting coaching right.

In the following chapters, we will explore the art and science of sales coaching by examining more closely who to coach, what to coach, and how to coach. In addition, we will provide a best practice checklist and some implementation ideas for making it happen.

Reflection Point 4

PAUSE FOR NOW AND COMPLETE THE EXERCISE ON PAGE 65

CHAPTER FIVE

Who to Coach

When it comes to determining who to coach, keep two overarching principles in mind.

One Size Does Not Fit All

If you are a Sales Leader with ten to twelve direct reports, each will have a different set of existing skills and different potential for personal development. So, the first important principle is to spend the appropriate amount of time with each person and to determine the specific focus for coaching. You cannot coach everyone on everything all at once. So, determine with the salesperson the one or two areas that will be the starting point for your coaching conversations. We advocate identifying and reinforcing both strengths and areas for development.

Allocating Your Time Is a Big Deal

There are two common pitfalls that sales leaders make when allocating their time to coaching. One is adding up the total number of days or hours they want to dedicate to coaching and dividing that time equally among the team. The second trap is overinvesting time in poor performers. We wouldn't recommend either.

In *Level Five Coaching System*, we provide frontline sales leaders with specific training on building 90-day coaching plans. They examine each salesperson on their team and decide what they want to coach and how much time they will dedicate to coaching to maximize the return on their coaching investment.

Just as you would prioritize your accounts as a salesperson, you should also prioritize your coaching time with your team. One bit of secret sauce in our model is not only considering how someone is performing against the plan but thinking about their knowledge and skill level and how receptive they are to feedback—what's their "coachability." These two dimensions can change the dynamic of time allocation and the ROI you yield from the coaching time spent. When prioritizing who your A, B, and C priorities are for coaching time, we suggest a 4:2:1 ratio. Therefore, you would spend twice as much time with you're A Group as your B Group and twice as much time with your B Group as your C Group. The exception, as we will discuss later, is the new hire. Initially, we give them an A Group priority.

With the above conditions in mind, and for purposes of discussion, we will notionally divide sales teams into the classic bell-shaped curve. There are three performance groups based on a normal distribution: low performers (16% of the team), average performers (68%), and high performers (16%).

Here, the literature is clear. Although there are exceptions, most sales leaders would suggest starting with that middle group of average performers then working with the other two groups—low and high performers. The reasons vary from, "The bottom and top groups are harder to coach," to "You get more bang for the buck with the middle group," to specific comments such as, "Some in the lower group may be in the wrong field."

Best practices related to what and how to coach all the groups will be addressed in subsequent chapters. There are, however, some special considerations for coaching low performers and high performers. In this chapter, let's turn our attention to those two groups.

Low performers. When it comes to coaching low performers it's important to distinguish whether someone is an underachiever—that is, their performance is low, but they have potential—or they are a poor performer in that their performance is low and they do not have much potential to improve.

A common trap is failing to distinguish an underachiever from a poor performer and perhaps overlooking a diamond in the rough. If they are a true underachiever, then the first step in the coaching process should be to determine whether the lack of performance is due to a skill deficiency or a motivational issue.

But what if the person is truly a poor performer? The trap with someone who is a poor performer is failing to identify that they are not well suited for sales and getting frustrated, ignoring the problem, or transferring the problem to a colleague. Here, the best practice is probably more about counseling the individual to reevaluate their career path than coaching them on how to improve their sales ability.

High performers. If you listen carefully to conversations among sales leaders and get the story behind the story, two rationales for not coaching high sales performers pop up. The first is a take on the old notion that if it's not broken, don't fix it. "My high performers are doing just fine, so I leave them alone—the main thing is to not mess them up." The second reason is, "They don't want to be coached."

When we interview clients who are high-performing salespeople about the nature of their sales leader's coaching, we ask how much time their leaders spend on coaching calls with them. The answers are often concerning. One seasoned salesperson said she had spent more time being recruited by the VP of Sales of their major competitor in the last six months than she had with her sales leader. Under-investing time with high performers can have negative consequences.

Assuming one is serious about coaching high sales performers, what are some specifics for getting it right?

- **Try innovative assignments.** High sales performers love challenges and enjoy trying new ways to address perplexing problems. Also, they can make tactical adjustments quickly and effectively.
- **Don't forget blueprinting.** It is a good idea to keep track of what and how these high sales performers do what they do. Many ideas can be translated into techniques that can be transplanted to the rest of the sales team.

- **Provide actionable feedback.** Contrary to popular opinion, high sales performers do want and appreciate feedback as long as the feedback is thoughtful, concise, and actionable. And, the really good news is they can implement it imaginatively and creatively.
- **Use multiple approaches and people.** Because high performers assimilate information quickly and reach a boredom plateau sooner than most, using all the resources available is a good coaching idea.
- **Solicit feedback.** Since high sales performers are good at doing what they do, they expect their ideas to be considered in formulating how the coaching takes place.
- **Provide recognition.** Not unlike the rest of us, high sales performers appreciate awards and recognition. Even though they have received many, it is still a good idea. In this case, the rewards can take on many different forms, such as the aforementioned innovative assignments.
- **Don't confuse confidence with arrogance.** There is little doubt that high sales performers are extremely confident. Sometimes if that confidence is viewed through the wrong end of the telescope, it can come across as arrogance; most of the time, it is not.

When considering who to coach, the middle 68% should be kept front-of-mind. However, one neglects high sales performers at their own peril. They are extremely intent on developing their sales skills and talents—if not with you, then somewhere else.

As a final topic in this "who to coach" discussion, let's examine one special population.

New and high potential. A special coaching challenge is presented when a leader has the good fortune to hire a new young salesperson they immediately recognize as someone with high potential.

High potential individuals are people who have special talents, unique capabilities, high motivation, and a sense of commitment that set them apart.

It is always sad news when people do not develop to their potential, but it is particularly criminal when the ones with high potential fail to do so.

Knowing what successful people do provides a sales coach with the information needed to help new high potential salespeople achieve the success they are capable of obtaining. Would they get there on their own? Sure, most would, but some might not. Plus, coaching can help them get there quicker with fewer mishaps along the way. Here are some specific coaching tips for this population:

Focus on being productive, not being busy. A sales leader can help a young high potential salesperson navigate the requirements, procedures, and paperwork that are inherent in any sales organization. Most things make no difference, so help a new high potential salesperson focus on things that matter.

Work outside the comfort zone. Many young high potential people are reluctant to accept an opportunity because they think they are not ready. One of the reasons for this is many high potential people tend to be perfectionists. Hence, they often feel they need additional knowledge and experience before they can accept a challenge. Consequently, they miss growth opportunities and, in some cases, develop a negative reputation for not being a go-getter.

Recognize the importance of other people. Any top-performing salesperson knows that one key to the success puzzle is leveraging human resources—do you know others who can help you be successful? Some of the others are sales colleagues; some are in other functions such as marketing and technical support. A good sales coach can introduce the right people at the right time, and consequently, impact the development of the new high potential salesperson.

Maintain a positive outlook and learn from mistakes. Even if you have a lot of potential, if you are a brand-new salesperson, it is fairly easy to get on a downer. Half of your first customer contacts don't call back, your first meeting gets canceled, and that account you were given as a "done deal"—well, it still is not done. This is where a coach can help.

Keep it simple. In sales, one can, in the wink of an eye, become overwhelmed with the amount of information available: product information, marketing data, pricing structures. And that is just the short list. A coach can help a new high potential salesperson separate the wheat from the chaff.

As a sales leader, if you are smart enough or lucky enough to have some new, young, high potential people on your team, take the time and effort to coach them to success. What they will be able to achieve in the long run is often startling.

Reflection Point 5

PAUSE FOR NOW AND COMPLETE THE EXERCISE ON PAGE 66

Chapter Six

What to Coach

In this chapter, we examine two increasingly important "What to Coach" challenges: virtual coaching and coaching universal sales performance.

Virtual Coaching

In today's virtual world, many sales leaders are called upon to coach video practice submissions from team members on virtual role-play platforms or recorded Zoom calls. In this case, they are viewing a recording of a salesperson practicing a skill. These platforms are useful for augmenting the precious little time sales leaders can dedicate to coaching call behaviors in the field.

As the sales leader, you have received a "performance gift." A salesperson on your team has submitted a video for your review. How do you provide constructive personal feedback that also supports your coaching culture and business development challenges? In most instances, the videos show a team member practicing a selling skill or describing how they will apply a strategy in an account. So why do we call it a "gift"?

The literature is clear. The best indicator of an authentic coaching culture, and the fastest way to promote one, is having team members actively seek feedback—that is, the salesperson asks for coaching help. The evidence suggests this is telling behavior of an organization where coaching is thriving.

Remember, most submissions you will receive are not the first take from the performer. On average, the person sending the video will rehearse that submission several times before sending it.

What's different about this type of coaching?

Typically, coaching involves a two-way conversation. Whether you're in person, on the phone, or engaged in an online meeting, you create a dialogue. By following a process of inquiry and discovery, you ask questions about the performance, and the performer offers their point of view. However, in virtual coaching, you're not engaged live with the performer. You are watching a recording and then recording an assessment of the submission. So, there is a need to do some things differently. For example, you don't have the advantage of asking questions and getting an immediate response. However, you can pose questions to prompt replies in another submission.

A few tips:

- The key is to keep your remarks simple, concise, and straightforward.
- Do not try to cover the waterfront or boil the ocean.
- Pick a few highlights and a few areas for improvement, if any, and be specific.

Although it varies somewhat by platform, there are generally three choices in completing your assessment of the video submission:

- **You can ask the performer to try again.** Maybe it's a single element of the skill model that was missing, or perhaps keywords you wanted to hear in a response were not used. It might not be the words but the music. In other words, there was an issue related to energy or tone of voice. Perhaps the salesperson was overly earnest, or the repeated "umms" and "ahhs" diminished the message.
- **You can close off that assignment and mark it completed.** If the job met your expectations and the submission suggests the performer understood the concepts and delivered a compelling response, then you can check that off the list and move on to another assignment. But remember, it's essential to reinforce the behavior you observed. A verbal pat on the back is always a good idea.

- **You can ask the performer for permission to add their submission to the leaderboard.** When you identify a "best in class" presentation, it's essential to share that with others on the team. Peer coaching is a potent form of feedback. By sharing the video with others, you multiply the value of that work and provide a way of recognizing the performer by indicating their work is exemplary.

How do you get it right?

When the performer is not present, it can be tempting to shortcut the process and provide the "good job" or "atta girl" or "atta boy" responses. After all, you are busy, and you have eight more video submissions to watch. Yet, we know that is not the best approach and can lead to a lack of interest in participating on both sides. Here we have a couple of suggested best practices.

As the leader, you should be familiar with the critical content that the performer was assigned.

If there is a skill model, you should know the steps so you can look for them in their response. As we wrote earlier in this chapter: "You can't coach it if you don't know it."

- If you are going to provide feedback to someone, knowing "what good looks like" is vital.
- Provide account examples that reflect the feedback you are providing.
- Being vague in your reply is not useful feedback.

Start with the merits, not the concerns.

Let's assume we have asked you to evaluate several math problems.

> 4 + 2 = 6; 9 - 5 = 4; 7 + 3 = 10; 12 - 4 = 8; 3 + 2 = 6; 5 + 5 = 10; 3 + 5 = 7

What do you think the average person often will say first when giving feedback? If you said that they got two wrong, you are right.

Most people will count the number of wrong answers as they review the work versus the number of right answers. It's human nature.

Every submission has a good idea or two. Even if it's a stretch to see something of value, the fact that the person completed the exercise is a plus. It's easy to point out the bad and overlook the good. But the purpose of itemizing the merits first is that it acknowledges the right behaviors and reinforces their use.

The trigger for you is to stop yourself when you are formulating your response and ask a simple question: "What did I like about this performance?" If you find you are disagreeing, ignoring, or rejecting someone's ideas or behavior, you know you haven't started with the merits.

Once you have your list of what you like, it's fair game to suggest a better way or another approach.

To reinforce, it's essential to be specific. Saying, "I wasn't comfortable with the way you said that" is not precise. It would help if you gave examples such as: "You may recall that the third step in managing the objection is to test your proposed solution to see if the customer is comfortable with the response. How about trying it again, and practice that step as part of your response?"

The close is essential.

Just as you would in a sales call, do a quick recap to close the feedback session.

- Thank the performer for their submission.
- Itemize the specific merits of their video.
- Suggest specific ideas or methods for improvement.
- Suggest next step: Try again, the assignment is complete, or seek permission to post to the leaderboard.

Coaching Universal Sales Performance Challenges

When asking the question "What to coach?" it's possible to formulate an answer by defining two performance domains.

One domain is about knowledge and skills. There are important topics on the knowledge side such as product knowledge, marketplace insights, and industry trends. Flipping to sales skills, you have the classic topics most training departments have been addressing for years—skill areas such as asking questions, active listening, handling objections, and closing.

A second domain consists of challenges that are more composite and personal. See if any of these examples seem familiar:

- Salesperson is not meeting their numbers.
- Salesperson is at the top of the stack rankings, but at the bottom of the popularity polls with the back shop and sales support staff.
- Salesperson isn't on board with selling the new product and prefers to take a wait-and-see approach before introducing it to their customers and prospects.
- Salesperson is consistently late with required expense reports and isn't logging activities regularly in the CRM.
- Salesperson is living off their existing accounts and not calling on new customers or expanding into new buying centers, yet they want to keep the large list of prospects.
- Salesperson's call activity is plummeting—the standard is two calls per day, and they barely make one per day.
- Salesperson has a pipeline full of opportunities, but they are all at low probability and stalled.
- Team selling is a new initiative for the organization, but the salesperson is reluctant to engage others.

These performance challenges are often thought of as difficult coaching conversations because they involve developing awareness and generating a positive path forward without hurting the salesperson's ego or making them defensive.

Let's take a look at some considerations and best practices that are particularly important for handling these universal types of sales performance challenges.

What's different about this type of coaching?

Importance of attitude and motivation. When it comes to coaching a sales skill like asking questions, there is not a major attitudinal or motivational barrier that needs to be overcome. Over the years, we have not encountered many salespeople having a significantly negative attitude about the art and science of questioning. Getting more proficient is indeed a straightforward skill development challenge.

On the other hand, coaching a salesperson to deal with an issue like being late with expense reports or taking a wait-and-see attitude about selling a new product will frequently involve surfacing and discussing issues that have a considerable attitudinal and/or motivational component.

Impact on others. A second difference is that a deficiency in many universal sales performance challenges tends to not only impact the salesperson in question but also with whom they may be working. For example, in companies where team selling is critical, the salesperson with a lone wolf "let me handle this" approach will impact not only their revenue but also the performance and behavior of others on the team. This characteristic tends to increase the criticality of the sales leader spending time on these types of issues.

Lack of alternative corrective strategies. There is no lack of training programs, e-books, and tools for getting better at handling objections or improving your active listening skills. There are far fewer resources for helping a salesperson develop a better attitude about the CRM system. One-on-one coaching is possibly the only viable approach for turning these types of things around.

How do you get it right?

Most of the ideas and skills necessary for doing a good job coaching universal sales performance challenges are also helpful for coaching traditional sales knowledge and skills. However, the following ideas and skills are particularly critical for coaching these universal sales performance challenges, and the ideas and skills need to be applied with somewhat more care.

Develop trust. Trust between the salesperson and the sales leader is critically important for all aspects of the relationship. However, it is particularly key when it comes to coaching a behavior that has a significant attitudinal and motivational component.

In the short run, a sales leader can demand compliance for solving an issue like late expense reports, but if a long-term answer is to be found, they must earn commitment, which requires trust. Believing that trust will just happen doesn't work. Sales leaders must make a conscious effort, devoting time and energy to developing trust. In that regard, there are no universal best practices; however, there are some actions that are worth exploring.

- **Be a filter, not a funnel.** Protect the salesperson from getting those "you have to do this right away" type of requests from everyone, all the time. As a sales leader, filter out the requests that can be put on the back burner, handled by someone else, or be dealt with by you. This establishes priority for the salesperson.
- **Share why.** If, for example, you are coaching the salesperson to change their behavior when dealing with other members of the team, help them understand why that is important for them and the rest of the team.

  Salespeople, like everyone else, have a propensity to stay in their comfort zone—doing more of what they are doing well. There are many reasons and rewards for taking up permanent residence in one's comfort zone, like being comfortable and successful with a given strategy and/or a fear of change.
- **Minimize the risks of failure.** Trying something different involves risks from perhaps an initially reduced commission to negative feedback from customers and peers. Where possible, the sales leader needs to help the salesperson manage and minimize these risks. Here, it is important

for the sales leader to understand the risks as perceived by the salesperson.

Salesperson assumes responsibility. One key component for coaching a challenge involving an attitudinal and motivational component is a determination to let the person being coached maintain responsibility for the solution.

So, how might a sales leader respond to a salesperson without taking over the problem? One possibility is to use questions that help the salesperson develop self-awareness of the challenge and why and how the challenge can be addressed. Questions like:

- What will happen if you continue to do what you're doing?
- What have you done so far to solve this?
- What else could you do about it?
- What do you know about why your colleague is responding that way?
- Do you think that will be true in the future?

Questions like these enlarge the range of actions that salespeople can consider. They take about the same length of time as giving advice or issuing an order, but they create the possibility that the person being coached will take a new tack, try a different approach, and keep at it. They reduce the chance that sales leaders will make it worse by jumping in and intervening. More importantly, they imply that the sales leader has confidence in the intelligence, good intentions, and capability of the salesperson.

A Final Thought

Somewhere along the path to achieving real change, most people need some help when trying out new behaviors and instituting new practices. The performance change journey can be frustrating, tedious, and sometimes even a little scary. After all, it's not easy to try new things, particularly when you are trying them out in front of customers. Everyone needs recognition and acknowledgment of their efforts along the way to results. Top-performing coaches understand this, and they not only help their salespeople get off to a good start in their change process, but they also continue to stand by to help them deal with attitudinal and motivational issues and the risks associated with the fear of failure.

Reflection Point 6

PAUSE FOR NOW AND COMPLETE THE EXERCISE ON PAGE 67

Chapter Seven

How to Coach

While most sales leaders agree about the importance of sales coaching, most also admit that the job isn't getting done. Many great companies start coaching initiatives with tremendous energy and commitment. Far fewer exit the other end of the tunnel.

Since it is more important than ever to have a superior sales team, achieving that goal is also more important than ever. Consequently, market-leading companies are placing a higher priority on coaching. Let's explore some of the how-to best practices for getting coaching right.

Giving Feedback—Addressing a Troublesome Barrier

Perhaps the ultimate cornerstone for effective coaching is the ability to provide feedback to the salespeople as to what they are getting right, what they need to improve, and what they should do about it.

But providing effective feedback is not a skill that comes easily. The old notion that some folks are just naturally good at providing feedback does not hold up very well under inspection. It is a composite skill that requires training and practice.

Let's take a look at getting it right, starting with one particularly troublesome barrier.

Although the number is somewhat speculative, about 30% of feedback is not received; that is, people don't take it seriously. Several reasons are driving this phenomenon. In some cases, the feedback isn't taken seriously because the recipient isn't willing to hear it. They believe it is incorrect or based on flawed observations, or they don't view the person providing the feedback as credible.

In other cases, the feedback is heard but ignored because it does not match the self-image of the recipient. They might have difficulty accepting their self-limitations, or they are resistant to any type of change. Or they may believe the feedback but don't have the innate ability to change, so they ignore the suggestions. If someone told the average golfer that they had to learn to hit a 300-yard drive or they wouldn't be successful at golf, most would ignore the feedback as they know they don't have the physical ability to do that.

Because of the complexity of this problem, there is no magic potion for a cure. However, the problem, regardless of the underlying reason, can be minimized if more time is spent up front with the sales leader and salesperson discussing the coaching process.

A good portion of this discussion should be devoted to where the salesperson is coming from. Topics such as:

- What do they think about the whole idea of coaching?
- What are their expectations surrounding feedback?
- What are their strengths, and what skill sets would they like to improve?

Improving the Diagnosis

How would you judge the truth of the following statement: Most people can accurately assess their own strengths and weaknesses? Unfortunately, it's not true.

Research highlights that most people struggle when attempting to construct an accurate self-assessment of their abilities. They have great difficulty pinpointing their strengths and weaknesses. In fact, most people tend to seek out evidence that confirms their positive opinions about themselves and to ignore evidence to the contrary. And unfortunately, many people hold on to their positive self-assessment even after their coach has provided them with contradictory feedback to that assessment.

It is very difficult to travel the performance improvement road unless everyone agrees on where the journey is beginning. Acknowledging the myth around the accuracy of self-assessments and achieving a better beginning diagnosis are two key steps for improving the coaching process. Some specific ideas for the coach are:

- Change the standard against which the salesperson is self-judging. For example, shifting to a best practice standard versus "what everyone else is doing" will help neutralize explanations for performance weaknesses.
- Be specific when describing behaviors such as "creating value" or "developing customer relationships."
- Respond to unlikely explanations for certain behaviors or lack of performance by pointing out how others facing the same challenge have been able to achieve the desired results.
- Help people depersonalize negative information to make it easier to confront and handle.
- Assign accountability. The traditional sales coaching model says, "I'm the leader. I'll suggest what you should do to improve your performance. Your job is to practice; my job is to give feedback." This model is about teaching people how to fix a performance problem. It often doesn't work because its objective is to teach something to someone rather than to help someone learn something. An alternative formulation that would shift the responsibility to the salesperson would be: "You're the accountable one. I'm responsible for helping you become more aware of your performance and expand your alternatives."

Getting the Right Start

What are some tips for the sales leader for planning their approach to providing feedback?

- **Recognize the difficulty of change**. Changing behavior is hard, even when you want to and have the ability. Therefore, it is best to focus on one composite behavior at a time (for example, asking questions or handling objections). Also, recognize that change is incremental. It doesn't happen overnight, and it needs to be reinforced along the way.

- **You can't coach it if you don't know it**. If you are going to provide feedback on sales skills, you have to know what skilled performance looks like. You don't have to have been the best salesperson ever, but you do have to know what constitutes top performance. As a leader, if there are areas where you are deficient, it is often helpful to leverage someone else in your group or company who can fill the void or work on the skill area yourself before you attempt to coach others.
- **You can know it and not know how to coach it**. Besides having sales expertise, sales leaders who are good at giving feedback to their sales team have learned to listen, display empathy, know how to develop trust, and have honed a process they're comfortable with to provide feedback. This is one of the reasons why the best salesperson often does not make the best coach; they know it, but they can't coach it because they never learned how to coach.
- **Balance matters**. Great coaches realize the importance of providing balanced feedback—both strengths and weaknesses. If a salesperson is particularly good at something, help them leverage that skill to accomplish new challenges.

On the other hand, some sales leaders at Level 1 and 2 have gotten the "you're good at that" feedback down pat, but they don't tackle areas requiring improvement. Granted, it can be hard. Difficult feedback can result in conversations laced with tension. However, avoiding areas requiring improvement and hoping for change is not beneficial for the salesperson. Salespeople often wonder if there are areas where they need to improve but don't know how to tackle the change, so the feedback is welcomed.

Leveraging Time

Although many players are important for an effective coaching effort, the pivotal job is the frontline sales leader. The problem is time or lack of it. Sales leaders do not have a lot of spare time. So, if coaching is to happen, the time issue must be wrestled to the ground. There is no magic solution, but a few ideas are to better leverage the time presently available, review where you are spending time, assess whether some of the tasks could be done by others or perhaps not done at all, and set a specific time commitment target.

You can also leverage the time available by utilizing online coaching. With the advances in learning management systems software, virtual coaching can be both efficient and effective.

- Individualize your coaching effort. If you are a sales leader with a team of ten to twelve salespeople, it is important to individualize your coaching effort to each member of the team. Some may need help building their call execution skills or their account strategy skills. Others may need help in leveraging an existing strength related to business acumen. It's why our 90-Day Coaching Planner provides you a snapshot of the strengths and developmental needs of each player on your team. That is why we encourage sales leaders to build a coaching plan for each member of their team each quarter. This is a snapshot in time of their strengths and the areas for development.
- Take advantage of training time. You don't have to build the training, but we strongly believe that you should participate in delivering it. Your sales enablement team would welcome your help. It speaks volumes to the participants when you are present. How many times have you attended a national sales training experience where the salespeople were in one room and the sales leaders stayed in another? A huge lost opportunity for coaching!

State-of-the-art sales training programs incorporate sales leaders as table leaders and coaches. In a training session where sales leaders serve as coaches, the amount of time devoted to coaching is greater than could be achieved in the field after months of effort. Providing feedback is challenging to learn and difficult to do, but participation in sessions like these is really important for mastering coaching. This is another way to make sure you don't get rusty.

Building a Coaching Model

Proposition. When it comes to providing coaching feedback, simple and immediate trump comprehensive and later.

Let's take a look at a scenario that dramatizes this comparison.

Scenario. A sales leader and one of her salespeople just got out of a sales call that beforehand had been designated a good coaching opportunity. The leader says, "I took a lot of good notes and have a number of suggestions. But as I look at my watch, I'm running late, and I have a busy day ahead, so why don't we just postpone the debriefing until this coming Friday before our sales meeting?"

Legitimately one can ask whether this questionable scenario ever really happens or is so rare that it doesn't matter. From experience and observations, we would suggest that if one hundred salespeople are assembled in a room and asked if that happens, more than a few would raise their hands.

There are some even worse versions of the scenario: The coaching day never gets scheduled in the first place, or the debriefing scheduled for Friday never happens, or (a particular favorite among salespeople) they get the coaching suggestions in an email.

Given that the scenario does happen, let's revisit our proposition and examine why now wins over later and simple beats comprehensive.

- **Opportunity lost.** Observations without feedback mean no coaching occurs, and unfortunately, that which is postponed until Friday often never happens. Postponing feedback, particularly if it frequently occurs, also conveys a subtle message about the overall importance of coaching.
- **Memory fade.** As the time between the call and the debriefing increases, the recall of the behavioral specifics tends to quickly fade, and a shared vision is lost. In the worst case, the coaching session turns into a "my memory versus your memory" discussion.
- **Feedback overload.** If you are on the receiving end of the feedback, the simple versus comprehensive point is a

big deal. One time, when John was traveling with a pharmaceutical company salesperson, she pulled out an 8 1/2 x 11 page on a clipboard, and on it were the items she was being evaluated on when she did ride-alongs with her sales leader. There had to be thirty items on the checklist. Many psychological experiments have shown that our short-term memory can hold only a limited number of separate items. The average is about seven items, plus or minus two, depending on the individual. Our point of view is to minimize the number of items you coach at any one time. Remember to list the merits of the performance, and choose wisely the one or two things you want to work on that quarter.

Positive feedback tends to be underutilized, and its power underestimated. Doing a better job in determining when and how to provide positive feedback can be another step toward improving sales coaching.

- **Asking questions**. A consistent theme emerges from a review of the best practice research on sales coaching. When top-performing sales leaders are asked what they've observed over the years as the key feature of great coaching, a pervasive answer is, "Ask more and talk less."

Great coaches withhold their opinions and solutions because they recognize, in the end, the best ideas often come from the person being coached. As one sales leader put it, "Effective coaches ask, listen, and then tell." The simple but powerful idea of ask, listen, and then tell applies across a wide spectrum of coaching situations—from call debriefs in the field to one-on-one coaching sessions.

Like most good ideas, ask, listen, and then tell is easy to say but difficult to do. Believing in the power of the idea is the first step, but the execution requires developing the skill set to ask the right questions.

Therefore, it is useful to adopt a common sales coaching language and common process understood by the sales leader and the salesperson for almost any coaching scenario. The specific coaching process adopted is not so important; a number of viable alternatives exist. The key is to pick one. As a jump-start, a simple and straightforward coaching language and process can be used by frontline sales leaders. Ours is described below.

The A.S.P.I.R.E.™ Coaching Model

A.S.P.I.R.E.™ is a practical problem-solving and decision-making coaching model to improve performance and achieve your desired accomplishments. It involves candor, inquiry, and listening versus telling. We have said this before, but it is worth repeating: Coaching shouldn't be about telling a performer you should do this or shouldn't do that. That interferes with their learning. For many sales leaders, using our A.S.P.I.R.E.™ model will require Levels One, Two, Three, and Four sales leaders to unlearn their current approach to coaching before they can truly apply the A.S.P.I.R.E.™ model. When one is coaching by telling, it leads to compliance. It's the key distinguishing characteristic between a Level Five sales leader and all other levels. Asking questions nurtures learning and leads to commitment. People will only tolerate our coaching conclusions, but they tend to act on their own conclusions. Your job is to help them formulate those conclusions.

"Performance is potential minus interference."

— *Tim Gallwey, The Inner Game*

The value of following discrete steps in a skill model is that it keeps the discussion on track, and the acronym is simple to understand, easy to remember, and repeatable. The A.S.P.I.R.E.™ model can also be learned and used by salespeople so they can more effectively engage in the conversation when seeking coaching from their sales leader. Plus, they can use the model when asked about coaching on a project team or mentoring a new hire. Many have said that A.S.P.I.R.E.™ can be used in both their professional life and their personal life to unlock potential, foster collaboration, and develop hidden potential talent while inspiring innovation.

Let's examine the A.S.P.I.R.E.™ skill model more closely.

Accomplish – Clarify the objective of the conversation.

- What do we want to try to accomplish?
- Is it a behavior, skill, or result we are seeking to achieve?
- How can the objective be stated in S.M.A.R.T. terms?
- How important is this accomplishment to you? Why bother?
- Can you quantify what this achievement looks like?

Status – Determine where they are today in the pursuit.

- How long have you been working on this?
- What progress has been made to date, if any?
- What actions have you taken thus far?
- What did you do that was particularly effective?
- What will happen if you continue to do what you're doing?

Problems – Find out what is preventing progress.

- Where do you feel stuck?
- What are you having the most difficulty with?
- Are there barriers or obstacles in your way?
- Are there tools or resources you need but don't have?
- Is something holding you back from acting?

Ideas – Solicit ways to achieve success.

- What ideas do you have to make this happen?
- What ideas have you tried already?
- What else? Are there other ideas we could brainstorm to achieve our results?
- How might you use your greatest strength?
- What if these don't work? What other options could you pursue?
- If you could start all over again, what would you do differently?

Realistic – Determine if the ideas are practical.

- What is your assessment of our chances of success?
- Do you feel those are reasonable actions for us to take?
- What is your mindset about this challenge? Have you any self-doubt or fear of trying this?
- Do you trust these actions are in our control?
- How could we test these ideas?

Execute – Develop an implementation plan.

- What are our next steps?
- What actions do we need to commit to in order to make that happen?
- What results should we expect from those actions?
- How will we know when we achieved success?
- What would that look like?
- What support do you need from me?

The final step is key and often not given proper attention. One significant purpose of using questions in coaching has to do with accountability. Ownership of the plan. The purpose of coaching is not only to help others improve their skills; the ultimate measure of the success of any coaching relationship is whether it drives sales results. To accomplish this, accountability must be an integral part of the coaching relationship and having a plan to execute and monitor results is paramount.

Wrap Up

Every salesperson, by their nature, has the desire to achieve success and accomplish great things. When the Level Five sales leader partners with their team members using the A.S.P.I.R.E.™ coaching model, they realize dividends that might otherwise be lost.

The odds increase in your favor that the desired accomplishments will be realized. When that happens, your performers' engagement rises, and their sense of pride in their work dignifies them and raises their aspirations even higher. In the end, leadership is about getting others who are willing to follow you. The Level Five sales leader taps into performers' desires to learn and grow and excel. There is no better way to build loyalty and stretch your team to not just meet but exceed their revenue goals.

Reflection Point 7

PAUSE FOR NOW AND COMPLETE THE EXERCISE ON PAGE 68

Reflection Points

Chapter One Reflection Point—The Level Five Sales Leadership Model

Okay, it's time to look in the mirror and assess your sales leadership style and skill as a recruiter, trainer, and coach. At the end of these exercises, you can develop a personal development plan.

Let's begin with your leadership style. Are you a Buddy, Parent, Boss, Coach, or Partner?

List the members of your sales team and indicate the Level Five leadership style you predominantly employ with each of them. Then ask yourself if they would answer the question the same as you did.

Sales team member	How I lead them	How they think I lead them

Look at the characteristics and traits of the Level Five leadership hierarchy on pages 11 through 14. List those you want to start doing more of, stop doing, or continue doing to build a partner relationship with your team.

Start doing more	**Stop doing**	**Keep doing**

Chapter Two Reflection Point—The Sales Leader as Recruiter

Rate your recruiting performance against the seven habits:

Habit	Extremely Effective	Very Effective	Moderately Effective	Slightly Effective	Not Effective At All
I am always recruiting.					
I partner with my sales recruiters.					
I have a recruiting pipeline that helps me retain talent and find new candidates.					
I have a strong bench of candidates I can call tomorrow if someone turns over.					
I practice my behavioral interviewing at least once a week.					
I use a valid sales assessment to add science to my decision to hire or not hire.					

Chapter Three Reflection Point—The Sales Leader as Trainer

Habit	Extremely Effective	Very Effective	Moderately Effective	Slightly Effective	Not Effective At All
I am a partner with Sales Enablement.					
I diagnose performance challenges before prescribing training solutions.					
I will reinforce and follow up a training program versus trying something new all the time.					
I customize the training we do in our business.					
I have individual training plans for my team versus one-size-fits-all.					
I deliver small, bite-sized learning initiatives over time versus once a year.					
We take the time to evaluate and measure the results from our training investments.					

Chapter Four Reflection Point—The Sales Leader as Coach

HABIT	EXTREMELY EFFECTIVE	VERY EFFECTIVE	MODERATELY EFFECTIVE	SLIGHTLY EFFECTIVE	NOT EFFECTIVE AT ALL
I believe we have a coaching culture.					
I prioritize coach-ing over all other "to-dos."					
I believe everyone can improve and needs coaching.					
I prioritize coaching over selling.					

Chapter Five Reflection Point—Who to Coach

Habit	Extremely Effective	Very Effective	Moderately Effective	Slightly Effective	Not Effective At All
I prepare a 90-day coaching plan each quarter.					
I allocate my coaching time using an A, B, C, and New Hire priority.					
I don't overinvest in non-performing salespeople.					
I don't ignore coaching my top performers.					
I invite others to help me coach my team.					

Chapter Six Reflection Point—What to Coach

Habit	Extremely Effective	Very Effective	Moderately Effective	Slightly Effective	Not Effective At All
I share a common language with my team on what a quality call looks like.					
I am certain to point out strengths as well as areas for development.					
I feel confident that I coach sales calls well.					
I feel confident that I coach sales strategy well.					
I feel confident that I can coach universal sales performance challenges.					

Chapter Seven Reflection Point—How to Coach

Habit	Extremely Effective	Very Effective	Moderately Effective	Slightly Effective	Not Effective At All
I feel confident giving feedback.					
I feel confident I can spot the knowledge, skills, and behaviors I need to coach.					
I provide timely feedback rather than postponing it.					
I focus on one or two things when I coach versus the waterfront.					
I have an "ASK" versus "TELL" coaching style.					
I feel confident I can follow the A.S.P.I.R.E.™ coaching model.					

Now that you have reviewed your Coaching Activity Profile report, it is imperative that you act and create a Coaching Action Plan.

Please use the template below to create your action plan. Select a maximum of three areas that you want to develop (a minimum of one existing strength and a minimum of two development areas) and then identify what you will need to do and what others will need to do for you to achieve your development goals.

ACTION ITEMS		**ACTIONS/RESPONSIBILITIES FOR ME TO BE A LEVEL FIVE LEADER**	
	DESCRIPTION	**MYSELF**	**MY SALES LEADER**
1		+ +	+ +
2		+ +	+ +
3		+ +	+ +
4		+ +	+ +

When you have completed your Action Plan, the next step is to ensure accountability. Share your action plan with your sales leader and ask them to not only contribute to your development but also hold you accountable for your action plan commitments.

Appendix

Level Five Selling Overview

What constitutes "excellence in selling" has evolved. Today, most companies are going through a transformational period. They are changing what they buy, how they buy, and what they are willing to pay for it.

Level Five Selling hierarchy. When buyers change how they buy, sellers need to change how they sell. The Level Five Selling hierarchy was designed as a framework for implementing sales force transformation initiatives to address that challenge.

Level Five Selling

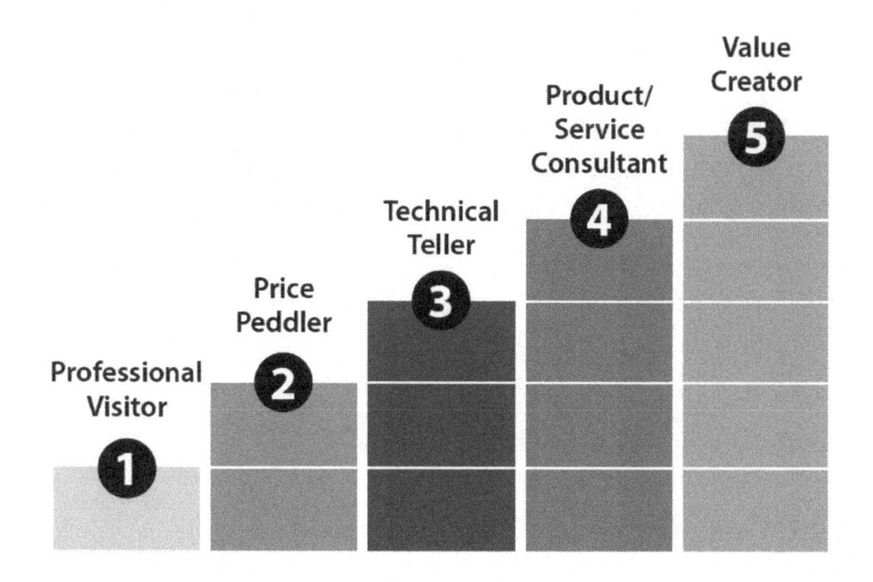

The Level One salesperson, a **Professional Visitor**, relies solely on the importance of relationships for achieving success. Of course, people buy from people they like, but it isn't the only reason they buy.

In Level Two, selling is all about price. The Level Two salesperson is a **Price Peddler**, who wins by selling the company's products at the lowest possible price. They turn their products or services into a commodity.

The Level Three salesperson, the **Technical Teller**, is all about telling the customer about the features of the product until they hit on something the customer likes. This is the old "spray and pray" idea that can actually create more objections.

Level Four is really the first level of professional selling. It goes beyond price peddling and feature pitches. The salesperson asks questions and thus uncovers and develops customer needs. Serving as a **Product/Service Consultant**, the Level Four salesperson addresses tactical problems, but they fall short of creating real value because they fail to connect a purchase to the broader strategic business picture.

The Level Five salesperson is a **Value Creator**. They look at the customer from both a business and a strategic perspective. They possess an in-depth understanding of their customer's industry and business. The customer views the Level Five salesperson as a trusted advisor providing both solutions and insights for driving business results.

Across markets, the days of the price peddler and the product teller are over. Customers want a trusted advisor, not a salesperson who just sells products. The key to becoming a trusted advisor is creating value.

How many Level Five sellers do you have?

The Case for Sales Coaching Redux

Over the past few years, there has been a lot of noise in sales productivity circles about the importance of sales coaching. Yet, it's been our experience that the actual depth and implementation of quality coaching has not lived up to all the hype.

We routinely survey salespeople about the coaching they receive from their sales leader. The data we gather continues to find that while many sales teams say they are providing coaching not many are truly instituting programs of measurable value.

Perhaps the most often stated, yet least measured, sales management performance standard is the percentage of time frontline sales leaders should spend in the field with their salespeople. We routinely ask senior sales executives about that number and, on average, they tell us that sales leaders should be in the field 50% of the time. Some even say it should be 80%. However, when we ask the frontline sales leaders to review their last 90-day calendars and report back their total number of days spent coaching in the field, we get percentages as low as 15%. Why such a discrepancy?

The most common response we get is a lack of time. Other priorities seem to fill their calendars leaving precious little time to see customers and ride shotgun with salespeople. Things like:

- Open territories they have to cover
- Internal projects they are assigned
- Firefighting a variety of issues like inventory outages
- Chasing down forecasts for senior sales management
- Meetings and training programs
- Managing the underperformers
- Onboarding new hires
- Recruiting to replace turnover
- And the catch-all "administrative paperwork"

Now to be fair, most of the sales leaders we meet tell us they would rather be out in the field, but somehow, they inadvertently get dragged into other things. The problem with field coaching is that it isn't something that is due on Friday at five o'clock. Forecasts are due, expense reports are due, but coaching plans are not. It's one thing to set an expectation, like spend two and half days a week in the field, but it's another thing to track and measure if it's being done and to follow through with a consequence if it isn't.

In following the old maxim that you have to inspect what you expect, we advocate for 90-day coaching plans turned in15 days ahead of each quarter. Those plans should specify what skills they will coach and how much time they will spend coaching each person on the team. Of course, there should be solid logic for their time allocation.

By getting your sales leaders out traveling more and coaching the salespeople in person, the team can yield major benefits.

The two extremes we see most often are sales leaders spending the majority of their time with the "problem children" or concluding that, say, if they have ten days and ten salespeople, then each salesperson gets one day. To prevent these types of situations, the coaching plans should be a part of the regularly scheduled one-on-one meetings with the sales leader. Just like the forecast is examined closely, the coaching plans should also be revisited regularly to gauge progress against plan.

Putting a discipline in place is important too, and it starts with buy-in. All sales leaders want to see their salespeople be successful, yet we think that some may not be totally bought into the notion of the payback. We know from Simon Sinek's acclaimed TED Talk, "How Great Leaders Inspire Action," that the "why" matters first when persuading others. To provide that context and to help win over sales leaders on the value of coaching, we offer a thought-provoking true-false exercise, one that you can test out with them in your next team meeting.

We call it The Case for Coaching.

Read the 12 statements about the benefits of sales coaching backed by various sources. Choose True or False.

		TRUE	FALSE
1.	Coaching Business Impact Sales coaching is the second most important tool for driving sales performance in companies.		

2.	More Time Coaching Sales leaders at high-impact (high-performing) sales organizations spend more time coaching.		
3.	Coaching Consistently +10% more salespeople achieve quota if you coach consistently.		
4.	Sales Coaching Drives Goal Attainment Salespeople who received just ten minutes of sales coaching a day enjoyed 17% higher goal achievement.		
5.	Focus on People, not Process Sales leaders who prioritize coaching over administrative duties perform identically to those who don't.		
6.	Coaching Increases Win Rates Having a dynamic coaching process increases sales opportunity win rates by 17%.		
7.	Coaching Maximizes Training Salespeople who received regular coaching from sales leaders after sales training achieved a productivity impact four times greater than salespeople who went through training with no follow-up.		
8.	Coaching Retains Sales Performers A study by the Corporate Executive Board shows that salespeople who received highly effective coaching from their sales leaders are far more likely to turn over than stay with their company.		
9.	Effective Coaches Outperform Direct reports of effective coaches outperform the direct reports of ineffective coaches.		
10	Coaching Importance vs. Execution Coaching is the activity that leaders perform least well.		

11.	Most Important Sales Activities Sales coaching is the second most important of the top four sales activities that impact overall sales effectiveness.		
12.	Ride-Alongs Alone Can Increase Sales Results Sales leaders traveling in the field can raise the productivity of salespeople by 25% within 18 months.		

By simply reading these statements, we find it stimulates interesting dialogue on a wide variety of sales leadership teams, often leading to problem-solving discussions about how senior sales leadership can remove some of the barriers currently stealing their time.

The bottom line is that we know the crucible for learning and skill development is on the job.

By getting your sales leaders out traveling more and coaching the salespeople in person, the team can yield major benefits. Here are a few examples of the outcomes we regularly observe:

- More quality deals in the pipeline and improved forecast accuracy
- Improved win/loss ratios
- More salespeople achieving and exceeding quota
- Shortened new-hire ramp time to full productivity
- Reduced turnover
- Increased customer satisfaction
- Improved product launch results
- Double or triple the amount of coaching
- Four to five times more practice and rehearsal of skills

ANSWER KEY

1. Coaching Business Impact

Sales coaching is the second most important tool for driving sales performance in companies.

Reality – False

A recent survey conducted by the Forum Corporation and The Sales Management Association of more than 200 companies, representing more than 500,000 salespeople, revealed coaching tops the list of investments that impact sales effectiveness the most.

Source: Forum

2. More Time Coaching

Sales leaders at high-impact (high-performing) sales organizations spend more time coaching.

Reality – True

High-Impact (high-performing) sales organizations prioritize sales coaching and are far more proficient at sales coaching than average and low-performing groups. They also spend more time coaching:

- 65% of sales leaders at high-impact organizations spend more than 20% of their time coaching
- 40% of sales leaders at low-impact organizations spend more than 20% of their time coaching

Source: Selling Power 2017 Sales Management Research Report

3. Coach Consistently

+10% more salespeople achieve quota if you coach consistently.

Reality – False

In fact, +30% more salespeople achieve quota if you coach consistently. Ways to coach consistently include:

- Meaningful coaching notes
- Low-friction feedback
- Clear goal-setting

Source: SalesForce, *Five Steps to Better Sales Performance*

4. Sales Coaching Drives Goal Attainment

Salespeople who received just ten minutes of sales coaching a day enjoyed 17% higher goal achievement.

Reality – True

Average District Goal Achievement correlated with Average Time Leader spends coaching each salesperson per month.

- Under 2 hours per month = 90% goal achievement
- 2-3 hours per month = 92% goal achievement
- Over 3 hours per month = 107% goal achievement

Source: *Building a Winning Sales Management Team: The Force Behind the Sales Force* (Zoltners, Sinha, and Lorimer; 2012)

5. Focus on People, Not Process

Sales leaders who prioritize coaching over administrative duties perform identically to those who don't.

Reality – False

There is a strong tendency for sales leaders to get pulled into administrative activities and away from coaching and mentoring salespeople. Sales leaders who prioritize coaching over administrative duties perform 5% better than those who don't.

- 75% of sales leadership believe their frontline leaders spend too much time on administration and logistics that don't add value to the business.

Source: SalesForce, *Five Steps to Better Sales Performance*

6. Coaching Increases Win Rates

Having a dynamic coaching process increases sales opportunity win rates by 17%.

Reality – True

Having a dynamic coaching process increases win rates to 59.1% versus 41.7% for organizations who leave coaching processes up to the sales leader. It also increases salesperson quota attainment to 61.5% from 53.4%.

Source: CSO Insights, *2016 Sales Enablement Optimization Study*

7. Coaching Maximizes Training

Salespeople who received regular coaching from sales leaders after sales training achieved a productivity impact four times greater than salespeople who went through with no follow-up.

Reality – True

According to research reported by the Corporate Executive Board, coaching is key to maximizing the value of sales training efforts. Without reinforcement, the average salesperson who takes a course will lose 87% of what they learned within a month.

Source: Sales Executive Council 2005 Teleconference Series "Building a World-Class Coaching Program," The Business Case for Sales Coaching, Hirevue.com

8. Coaching Retains Sales Performers

A study by the Corporate Executive Board showed that salespeople who received highly effective coaching from their sales leaders were far more likely to turn over than stay with their company.

Reality – False

Likelihood to stay at company was consistent across all levels of salesperson performance, from low to average to high. This is extremely important because replacing an average salesperson can cost between two and three times their base salary. The cost of replacing a high performing salesperson can also be between eight and ten times their base salary. The study showed that those who receive highly effective coaching from their sales leaders were far more likely to stay!

Source: Sales Executive Council 2005 Teleconference Series "Building a World-Class Coaching Program," The Business Case for Sales Coaching, Hirevue.com

9. Effective Coaches Outperform

Direct reports of effective coaches outperform the direct reports of ineffective coaches.

Reality – True

Direct reports of effective coaches outperform the direct reports of ineffective coaches by 25% and are 40% less likely to leave their organization.

Source: Corporate Executive Board

10. Coaching Importance vs. Execution

Coaching is the activity that sales leaders perform least well.

Reality – True

While coaching is both the sales leader activity most closely associated with salesperson success and the key to maximizing value of training efforts…it is, regrettably, also the activity that sales leaders perform least well.

Source: 2005 Sales Executive Council Research, "Your Business Case for Investing in coaching" Study of 450 Heads of Sales and 2,400 Salepeople

11. Most Important Sales Activities

Sales coaching is the second most important of the top four sales activities that impact overall sales effectiveness.

Reality – False

Sales Coaching is the most important of the top four sales activities that impact overall sales effectiveness. Most important sales activities that impact overall sales effectiveness:

1. Sales coaching
2. Salesperson training
3. New customer acquisition
4. Cross-selling/up-selling

Source: Forum

12. Ride-Alongs Alone Can Increase Sales Results

Sales leaders traveling in the field can raise the productivity of salespeople by 25% within 18 months.

Reality – True

"Instead of issuing a series of sales directives, as had been their custom, managers rolled up their sleeves and led a series of in-person sessions and ride-alongs. By targeting specific skills and enforcing their use with concrete goals, sales leaders raised rep productivity by 25% within 18 months."

Source: McKinsey & Company

Acknowledgment

People often ask us how we decided on our book's tagline. First, we brainstormed more than half a dozen ourselves, and then we surveyed over forty colleagues in the business for their opinion.

We had a great response, and we learned a lot. And then I got a call from Bob Potter, a seasoned sales consultant, with whom I have been friends (golf buddy) for some time. Bob wrote the book *Third Level Selling* long before mine. He's a Stanford MBA and ex-McKinsey consultant, and I've always enjoyed his company and counsel.

He asked some very thought-provoking questions, which is what consultants do. He said his experience is that people are more likely to avoid pain than find pleasure. I had heard that before in a sales training program, and it's called building the F.U.D. (Fear, Uncertainty, and Doubt) of the consequences of not acting.

Bob asked:

Q: What problem are you trying to solve?

A: We believe that high-performing sales leaders do not focus on the three strategies that significantly increase their odds of consistently meeting or exceeding quota. They spend their time doing other nonproductive things that don't grow revenue.

Q: What will happen if they don't focus on these three things?

A: They stand a good chance of not meeting their quota. In fact, it is almost a certainty.

Q: What is the implication for the Chief Revenue Officer who is likely to pay for your training?

A: They will not make their quota!

Q: Are you are trying to "close the quota gap" that exists in over 80% of sales teams?

A: I am.

Bob says: There's your tagline.

The other consistent feedback from the survey was that many people (one exception) liked the words "field-tested" a lot, suggesting the advice was proven and realistic and not something we made up in our basement.

So, the new tagline is:

Field-Tested Strategies to Close the Quota Gap!